Copyright © 2024

Written and illustrated by Samantha Finn

All rights reserved. No part of this book may be reproduced or used in any manner without the prior written permission of the copyright owner, except for the use of brief quotations in a book review.

CHICO'S UNDER THE SEA ADVENTURE

...the beach!

As Chico was walking on the sand, he saw a beautiful mermaid out in the sea..

He had never met a real mermaid before, so he knew he was going to have the best adventure!

'Of course I am, silly! I'm Molly', said the mermaid whilst giggling at Chico's question.

'Of course, you will need something
to dive under the sea in though',
she said.

Once Chico hopped into his submarine, he went deep into the sea ready for his adventure with Molly.

Chico went deeper...

...and deeper...

... until he finally caught up with Molly who was talking to her friend, Orla the octopus.

Chico was so shocked by Orla, 'You have so many legs, you must be a really fast swimmer', laughed Chico.

Orla swam up close to the submarine and said, 'I am very fast at swimming and because I'm so squishy I can fit into the smallest of places!'.

Chico followed Orla, who wanted to show him where she lived.

As Chico and Molly carried on with their adventure, they came across a very sad little sea horse.

'What's wrong little guy?', asked Molly.

'There he is!', shouted Chico, 'He was playing hide and seek!'.

And so, with the baby sea horse found, the adventure continued.

As the fish swam away, Chico could not see Molly anymore, he was scared he would get lost and never find his way back to the beach!

'Yes, I don't know how to get home', cried Chico.

Chico took a deep breath in and set off in search of home.

Chico went back past the rocks where he helped the sea horse.

He went past Orla the octopus' house.

He then came across a little dolphin dancing along and asked, 'Excuse me, do you know the way to the beach?'.

After a short while, Chico made it back to the beach where he found Molly waiting for him.

'I was worried you wouldn't find your way back', said Molly.

'Me too, but someone told me to stay calm when I was scared and I found my way back, thank you for the adventure and showing me your world', said Chico.

I wonder what Chico will get up to next...

Printed in Great Britain
by Amazon